LFC
Annual 2008

Written by Paul Eaton

A Grange Publication

£6.99

Contents

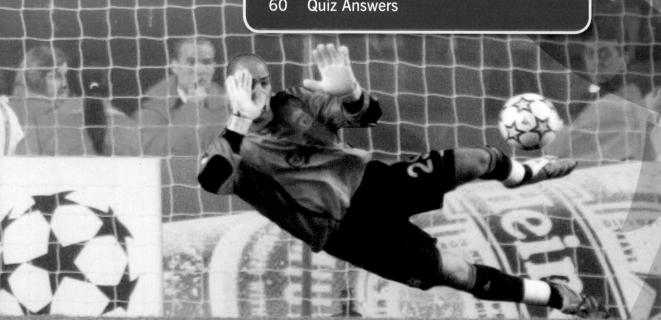

Introduction

2007 was another momentous year in the history of Liverpool Football Club.

The club was transferred into different hands following the takeover by Tom Hicks and George Gillett, stunning new plans for a brand new Anfield were revealed, the Reds smashed their transfer record by bringing Spanish star Fernando Torres to the club and we reached our seventh European Cup final.

Throughout this year's LFC annual we'll reflect on the highs - and the lows - of the last twelve months and speak to the men who have made the headlines at Anfield.

From the new owners to Rafael Benitez and the players, we've got every angle covered in this year's exciting annual.

Season Report
2006-07

August

After lifting the first trophy of the season thanks to a 2-1 Community Shield victory over Chelsea in Cardiff, the Reds quickly put their first Premiership point on the board as Robbie Fowler netted from the penalty spot to secure a 1-1 draw at newly promoted Sheffield United. Rafael Benitez then had to turn his attentions quickly towards the second leg of the 3rd qualifying round of the Champions League, but Israeli side Maccabi Haifa had no answer to the Reds and went down 3-2 on aggregate over the two legs.

Liverpool's first league victory of the campaign was sealed at Anfield against West Ham as Daniel Agger netted one of the goals of the season in a 2-1 success.

September

The Merseyside derby was next up for Liverpool and it was an afternoon to forget for the red half of the city as an Andy Johnson inspired Everton side cruised to a 3-0 victory at Goodison. The Reds first proper European game of the season followed at PSV Eindhoven and despite dominating most of the match, they had to settle for a point in a goalless stalemate.

The following weekend saw Didier Drogba score a wondergoal to send LFC crashing to an undeserved 1-0 defeat at Stamford Bridge as Chelsea made amends for their Community Shield loss.

Liverpool got back on track quickly and put together a run of three straight wins, with home victories coming against Newcastle and Tottenham in the league before Galatasaray were edged out in a 3-2 thriller as LFC went to the top of Champions League Group C.

Unfortunately the month ended on a low note as Bolton scored a goal in each half to record a 2-0 win at the Reebok.

October

After a lengthy break for international football, Blackburn frustrated the Reds and became the first side to leave Anfield with a point in a 1-1 draw. While the league form was patchy in the early months of the campaign, Liverpool had clicked into the groove in Europe and Peter Crouch's only goal of the game in Bordeaux maintained their superiority in the group.

Having already lost on the road to Chelsea, Everton and Bolton, it was Manchester United next up for Liverpool and sadly the same scenario unfolded again as strikes from Paul Scholes and Rio Ferdinand did the damage.

LFC recovered from the setback, however, and after disposing of Reading in the Carling Cup, Dirk Kuyt, Peter Crouch and Luis Garcia were all on target as they picked up three more Premiership points at the expense of Aston Villa.

Days later the Reds had all but sealed their qualification into the knock-out stages of the Champions League as Steven Gerrard netted his first goal of the season in a 3-0 home rout over Bordeaux.

Season Report
2006-07

November

November was an up and down month for the Reds but it began promisingly enough with a comfortable league victory over Reading and our Carling Cup adventure continued thanks to a Daniel Agger strike at Birmingham.

Their form on the road in the league wasn't getting any better though and after Arsenal had given LFC a heavy 3-0 defeat at the Emirates, they then had to be content with a point from a disappointing goalless draw at Middlesbrough.

Victory over PSV at Anfield ensured Liverpool would progress in Europe as group winners while Steven Gerrard was on the mark again in a slender 1-0 victory over Manchester City.

Frustratingly, the month ended with a goalless draw at home to Portsmouth who, at that stage of the season, were flying towards the top of the table.

December

With more than four months of the season having passed, the Reds finally secured their first away victory in the league with a 4-0 drubbing of Wigan at the JJB Stadium. Craig Bellamy (2), Dirk Kuyt and a Lee McCulloch own goal gave them the points in emphatic style.

LFC's first European loss of the campaign followed soon after but it mattered little as, on the team's return to the Ataturk Stadium, they lost 3-2 but still held on to top spot in Group C. Barcelona were to be Liverpool's opponents in a daunting looking last sixteen fixture.

Fulham, Charlton and Watford were all well beaten in an impressive series of league performances before Benni McCarthy ruined the Reds' Christmas with a Boxing Day winner at Ewood Park.

2006 ended in style for Rafa Benitez though as Luis Garcia popped up with a crucial strike to settle the game at Tottenham.

January

Liverpool opened 2007 in fine fashion with a comprehensive 3-0 success over Bolton with Peter Crouch, Steven Gerrard and Dirk Kuyt all on target.

There was little sign of the week which was to follow at that point, however, with two games looming against Arsenal in the two domestic cup competitions.

It turned out to be the worst spell of the campaign for the Reds as Arsene Wenger's men triumphed with a 3-1 victory in the FA Cup and then ran riot in the Carling Cup, running out 6-3 winners in front of a disbelieving Kop.

The Reds had to get back on the rails quickly to keep their season alive and Watford were well beaten the following weekend by three goals to nil.

Next up was the visit of Jose Mourinho and his champions but Liverpool simply blew Chelsea away with a dazzling display of football as Dirk Kuyt and Jermaine Pennant scored the goals to leave the Londoners singing the blues.

A precious 2-1 victory at West Ham followed as fans started wondering whether it was too late to mount a serious title challenge in the second half of the season...

Season Report
2006-07

February

Those thoughts were all but dashed within a couple of weeks as Liverpool battled to a goalless draw with Everton at Anfield and then saw their away day problems strike again as they dominated the match at Newcastle, but went down to a 2-1 defeat.

It was a different story in Europe, however, and the Reds sent shockwaves across the continent with a magnificent performance and result in the Nou Camp as goals from Craig Bellamy and John Arne Riise wiped out Deco's opener and secured an incredible victory at the home of the defending champions.

As if buoyed by their tremendous display in Spain, Sheffield United were sent packing in emphatic fashion at Anfield as goals from Robbie Fowler (2), Sami Hyypia and Steven Gerrard secured a 4-0 victory.

March

Two home games followed against Manchester United and Barcelona. Both matches were lost, but both generated vastly different emotions at the final whistle.

John O'Shea netted a last minute winner for Alex Ferguson's men at the Kop end as United maintained their assault on the league title, but Eidur Gudjohnsen's winner for Barcelona mattered little as Liverpool moved into the last eight of the Champions League on the away goals rule.

Back in the league the Reds laboured to a 0-0 draw at Aston Villa before picking themselves up to produce arguably their greatest league display of the season as Peter Crouch netted a hat-trick in a 4-1 thumping of Arsenal.

Season Report
2006-07

April

Goals from Steven Gerrard, John Arne Riise and Peter Crouch gave us a seemingly unassailable 3-0 lead from the first leg of our Champions League quarter final clash with PSV Eindhoven in Holland, and the result was confirmed the following week as Crouch netted again to guarantee a semi-final meeting with Chelsea.

The league programme continued with Reading, Middlesbrough and Wigan all being defeated at Anfield before Portsmouth took advantage of playing the Reds in between the Chelsea double header and secured a 2-1 victory.

In the first leg of the Champions League semi-final it was Chelsea who struck first as Joe Cole netted the only goal of the game at Stamford Bridge to leave Jose Mourinho and his men 90 minutes away from the final.

May

For the second time in three seasons, however, the Anfield crowd played their part in sealing the Reds' passage to the Champions League final as Daniel Agger netted to level the scores in normal time and then Dirk Kuyt fired home the winning penalty in the shoot-out to send the crowd into ecstasy as Liverpool celebrated their place in the final against AC Milan in Athens.

In the Premiership Fulham secured their Premiership safety with a 1-0 win at Craven Cottage and then Charlton took a point from Anfield in the final league fixture of the season, but one point was enough to secure Liverpool 3rd place in the league.

Unfortunately, the final didn't live up to the game between the two teams in Istanbul and the Reds dreams of lifting a sixth European Cup were dashed in the ancient city as goals from Filippo Inzaghi in each half helped Milan to victory at the Olympic Stadium. Dirk Kuyt offered hopes of a comeback with a goal late on, but for this year it just wasn't to be for Liverpool in the biggest competition of them all.

Rafael Benitez

Interview

Liverpool boss Rafael Benitez has a simple message for his players during the course of the 2007/08 season: "Show you're good enough to be Champions."

The Anfield manager knows the expectations at the club surrounding a possible title challenge are higher than ever following the summer investment into his playing squad, but he's keen to ensure his players focus on the age old 'one game at a time' philosophy in a bid to gain the winning momentum to carry them through the campaign.

"It's another big year for us and I want to see more improvement," he said. "We have to be careful that we don't talk too much because the only thing that matters is getting things right on the pitch.

"I am happy we have a better squad than last season and I'm happy with the players we brought in over the summer, but the key thing for everyone is to work as hard as possible every day, learn from the training sessions during the week and then play well and get the results we want during the matches.

"I know we have improved but you look around the Premier League and other clubs have improved as well. The Premier League is a difficult league to win and it will be another big battle for all the teams this year. Our aim has to be to challenge and for the players to show they can perform consistently over a difficult ten month season.

"We have proved in Cup competitions that we can beat any side on our day, but it's a completely different challenge to repeat that in the league. It's a different competition, a different style of football and it brings up different challenges, but I'm confident we can cope and that we'll have a good season."

"We have a plan and a long term vision here that we all believe in,"

The Liverpool boss is now in his fourth season at Anfield and despite constant rumours that he's set to leave for La Liga, he insists he is happy to stay because he believes the future is bright on the red half of Merseyside.

"We have a plan and a long term vision here that we all believe in," he added. "We know what we want to achieve and we know how to get there but sometimes these things take time.

"It's never easy to win any trophy in football and so we can be pleased with what we have achieved recently. To reach two European finals in three years was fantastic and I'm sure people from all over the world are now looking at Liverpool and realising that we are a good side. We have won trophies and progressed, but we still have some way to go.

"The key is always the players and I am sure we have a good group here. We have good experienced players and young boys who will all have a part to play in our future."

Before the summer signings arrived at the club, Benitez was quick to secure the services of established stars Steven Gerrard, Jamie Carragher, Pepe Reina and Xabi Alonso on new long term deals.

And it's these players he hopes will become the spine of the side as the Reds look to move to the next level.

"It's clear you have to keep your best players if you are going to do anything and we realised there were a number of them who we needed to speak with," he said. "It was important to get the contracts sorted early in the summer and I'm pleased there were no problems.

"The first deals we finalised were for Stevie and Jamie. Both wanted to stay at the club. They have a passion for this club and you can see that in the way they play. They are 100% committed to Liverpool and now they can be 100% focused on their futures at Anfield.

"I think the deals sent out a key message. Other players will look at Stevie and Carra committing their future to Liverpool and understand that this means we are determined to progress on the pitch.

"When we talk to players we'd like to sign for this club, we can point to the fact that they will be playing alongside the likes of Stevie and Carra.

"The same applies for Pepe and Xabi. With Pepe's age we knew we had to sort out a long contract quickly and as far as Xabi was concerned there was interest from other clubs but we were always clear that we didn't want to sell him.

"I am convinced that we have a bright future to look forward to. We need to be careful in terms of making predictions but there's no doubt we have the quality and the ability within the playing squad to be successful. It's going to be another long season for all the clubs involved in the league and we want to go out every week and give ourselves the best possible chance of achieving what we all desire."

And Benitez insists the club's loyal and passionate followers will again have a big role to play as the season progresses.

"I say it regularly but we have got the best fans in the world," he said. "At Anfield they are always like an extra player for us, especially in the big games, and when we go away from home we always know they will be there in their thousands to support us.

"We have given them some days and nights to enjoy over the past few years but we're not going to sit back now and reflect on that. We want to keep moving forward and keep looking to give them more trophies and more medals."

Liverpool's Magnificent Seven
From the 2006-07 campaign

1. Daniel Agger v West Ham – Premiership

It was Agger's first goal for the Reds and what a way to open his account as he collected the ball midway inside the Hammers' half of the field and strode forward before unleashing a crackerjack of a shot with his left foot which sent the ball arrowing into the top corner of the Kop net.

2. Jermaine Pennant v Chelsea – Premiership

With the Reds already a goal to the good against the Champions, Pennant doubled Liverpool's lead with a scorching volley from outside the area which dipped wickedly over Petr Cech before nestling nicely in the back of the Anfield Road goal.

3. Xabi Alonso v Newcastle – Premiership

Another Xabi special from inside his own half of the pitch as, with Newcastle goalkeeper Steve Harper out of position, the Spaniard fires a long range attempt which finds its way into the back of the net after Harper had slipped in a desperate attempt to keep the ball out.

4. Peter Crouch v Bolton – Premiership

A tight game was ensuing against Wanderers before Crouch finally broke down a resolute Bolton defence with a brilliant bicycle kick which crashed into the back of the Kop goal past a well beaten Jussi Jaskelainen.

5. Peter Crouch v Arsenal – Premiership

Crouchie netted his first hat-trick for the Reds against the Gunners on one of our best Anfield afternoons of the season, but his third was the pick of the bunch as he danced his way past the Gunners' defence before slotting the ball home to secure the match ball.

6. Steven Gerrard v Bolton

Steven Gerrard's managed to score some corkers over the season. This one against Bolton secured the points for the Reds as he volleyed home from the edge of the box in great style.

7. John Arne Riise v Tottenham

Another special from the left foot of our Norwegian full back as he blasts a vicious drive from outside the box which gives Paul Robinson no chance and results in the ball bulging the far corner of the Kop goal.

Word Search

Find Them All! Answers on pages 60-61

```
N  N  N  G  F  M  C  M  A  N  A  M  A  N  F  C
K  F  S  K  F  T  N  A  H  G  A  L  L  A  C  H
C  K  H  J  D  A  L  G  L  I  S  H  D  N  C  A
R  M  A  K  G  L  T  L  H  Q  L  K  L  M  L  M
J  E  N  Z  K  D  U  B  L  A  R  R  E  T  H  P
W  S  K  X  R  H  E  B  W  G  A  P  I  N  R  I
B  I  L  T  G  N  E  R  N  A  F  K  F  D  M  O
M  I  Y  F  I  W  E  C  L  A  R  T  N  L  P  N
D  R  O  T  O  N  X  E  N  C  T  R  A  V  T  S
R  V  E  W  S  W  B  N  M  E  L  S  H  S  U  R
A  Z  B  O  E  B  L  O  X  Z  M  M  I  M  L  K
R  J  N  N  O  N  S  E  D  W  L  E  T  N  K  B
R  L  M  R  Z  N  B  K  R  V  M  M  L  W  X  C
E  V  G  M  O  R  E  H  G  A  R  R  A  C  P  J
G  F  N  L  W  K  V  M  J  Z  R  R  B  O  R  G
L  L  A  J  H  A  N  S  E  N  G  K  K  R  P  B
```

Alonso	Champions	Grobbelaar	McManaman
Anfield	Clemence	Hansen	Owen
Benitez	Dalglish	Istanbul	Riise
Callaghan	Fowler	Kop	Rush
Carragher	Gerrard	Lawrenson	Shankly

Spot The Ball

Using your skill and judgement can you say where the ball is?
Answers on pages 60-61

19

New Owners
Tom Hicks &

2007 will always be remembered at Anfield as the year when the ownership of the club changed hands as George Gillett and Tom Hicks joined forces to buy David Moores' majority shareholding. This was their first interview after assuming control at Anfield.

First of all, why Liverpool Football Club?

George Gillett: Firstly, we're not going to pretend to be the most knowledgeable of Liverpool fans because that's clearly not true. I can say, though, that our families are big football supporters. We have been watching European football for several years.

Tom Hicks: I have been in the sports business for 12 years and with 162 baseball games and 82 hockey games a year, I was not looking for another team. George called me and explained what he thought was the vision and the opportunity at Liverpool. I have followed the English Premier League from afar because some of my business friends are ardent fans of the game. When I looked into this I was awe-struck with the history and the true passion of the fans compared to other sports I am involved with. The Texas Rangers have been around for 36 years and the Dallas Stars have been around for 13 years, so to have a chance of getting involved with a team with more than a hundred years of history and with fervent fans is something which really excited me. After a couple of weeks I told George I was seriously ready to be his partner.

George Gillett: Tom and I have been involved in sports for a long time. When you sit in our little country you get an unusual perspective and probably an incorrect one, because we think our sports are pretty popular. Then you come over here and see the tribal aspects of the fans and their affection and support for the team and realise it's a game which is watched by billions. You quickly see this is the most popular sport in the world and that this is one of the most popular clubs in the world. To have the opportunity of getting involved in this is a rare privilege.

George Gillet

The reason any businessman goes into sport is because they have a passion for winning. Despite all the success I've had in life, nothing has given me more satisfaction on an emotional level than winning the Stanley Cup in 1999 and being able to get my hands on the trophy. At that moment my smile touched both ears.

What do you hope to achieve with Liverpool Football Club?

George Gillett: We had the privilege of spending some time before the official announcement with Steven Gerrard and Jamie Carragher and they delivered us the message. They are all about winning and all about the passion from the fans. They asked us three specific questions:

They wanted continuity of management with David and Rick. They have enormous regard for them. They also spoke extremely warmly about Rafa and made us aware that they feel this man is truly one of the great geniuses in the recent history of the sport. They wanted to communicate to us the feeling from the dressing room was of great respect for the management team.

Secondly, they wanted to talk about players and to encourage us to support Rick and Rafa's efforts in building the team.

They were also clear with their views on the stadium. They made us aware the sound, the energy and the passion that Anfield provides needs to be incorporated into the design of the new stadium.

They were the three messages they wanted us to hear and we heard them loud and clear.

You were determined to get hold of this football club, weren't you?

George Gillett: We were. I think both Tom and I have learnt that it's a great honour and a rare privilege to be considered to hold one of the greatest assets in sport in trust. To have that privilege is really special.

It's a well managed club but we believe we bring some experience which the management can draw on to make things even better. Tom and I are a little put off that people assume everything is about money, because we really hope we have some ideas as well as some capital.

Tom Hicks: We have both been involved in building and modifying new stadiums so we think we can bring a lot of good ideas to the work which has already been done which will be to the benefit of the fans and the club.

New Owners
Tom Hicks &

I don't know how to properly communicate how much care David Moores put into making this decision. He questioned us aggressively about our commitment, our passion and our willingness to help take the club forward. He wants to ensure we can re-emerge as the greatest team in the Premier League and be fully competitive in Europe. The interview process was rigorous, it was not foregone and it was not about money. It was about our passion and our understanding of the fans of this club.

David is an amazing man and this club is his life. This was the most difficult decision of his life because every single fibre in his body is in this club.

Tom Hicks: This club has been in David's family for fifty years and when we left his house it was a very poignant moment because there were tears in his eyes. He agreed to be a Life President at the club and he will still be sitting in the directors' seats at Anfield. From the players' point of view, the best thing that can happen is that they feel nothing has changed except for a new stadium being built and more aggressive support in the transfer market.

George Gillett: The less the fans see any change the better for this club. Neither Tom or I are high-profile. We are both hugely supportive of our families and of our franchises but the less people write about us and the more they write about the fans, the challenges and the opportunities then the better for everybody.

It sounds like David really put you through it in terms of making sure you were the right people to take over...

George Gillett: Very much so. There were two processes and ultimately he had to make two difficult decisions. The club felt they had two very well qualified potential buyers and it's no secret that one had extraordinarily deep pockets whereas ours are deep but not that deep. I think they correctly chose the other party and we were not offended by that.

George Gillet

On the other hand, if there's any trait that the Gillett's and the Hicks have then it's patience and stubbornness. In hockey we have a saying that it's really tough to score if you're not in front of the net. We stayed in front of the net and we tried not to do anything which was offensive or negative. We wanted to reinforce our respect for what David and the team had built and ultimately we were given a second chance because the Hicks joined us. There's no doubt that we increased our price because they were with us and enabled us to have the capital to be more aggressive.

Can we bring the title here under your ownership?

George Gillett: I really hope so. Rick has told me of a Shankly saying that 'first is first and second is nowhere' and that sounds good to us.

"David is an amazing man and this club is his life. This was the most difficult decision of his life because every single fibre in his body is in this club."

23

Liverpool FC Unveil

On Wednesday 25 July 2007 Liverpool Football Club unveiled stunning new designs for their stadium in Stanley Park, coinciding with the submission of the official planning application to Liverpool City Council. We speak to Chief Executive Rick Parry about the new stadium and also get the views of some players.

LIVERPOOL FOOTBALL CLUB   SOUTH EAST VIEW

Rick, we were told the club would deliver the best stadium for the best fans – you've succeeded, haven't you?

Rick Parry: It's very, very exciting. The plans are a tribute to the commitment of the new owners George Gillett and Tom Hicks. When they took over they understandably wanted to review the stadium because they were concerned about the capacity and they wanted to see if we could produce something better. I think it's been worth the wait.

So talk us through the design – it's unlike anything we've ever seen before...

For me there are three key things. One is the Kop which is very much the heartbeat of the new stadium so we've very much got the tradition in that sense. There'll be eighteen thousands seats, it'll be steep raked and densely packed. We really wanted to get back as close as we could to the real heyday of the Kop.

Secondly, it's uniquely Liverpool. Nobody will look at this and mistake it for anything else. Anybody anywhere in the world will look at this stadium and say 'that must be Liverpool' which is a huge plus point.

And, remembering its setting, it's also been specifically designed for the park. It's very much a stadium of the park, it's not just in the park. It's been designed with the topography of the park in mind, showing great respect for its setting, but it's also captured the essence of English football stadia which tend to be asymmetric simply because they have grown up over time. Stands tend to develop at different times and so you end up with something that is definitely not a bowl shape and I think we have been able to recapture that but in a way which fits and works and provides a spectacular modern design. Full tribute is due to architects HKS who have really blended the things that matter to us and the traditions that matter to Liverpool with a spectacular piece of modern design.

24

New Stadium

How important was it to have the Kop as the centrepiece of the stadium?

It's something that we emphasised. I went out to meet the architects in Dallas and I emphasised how important the Kop was and so that was really the whole starting point for the stadium. Then when George and Tom came to see the game against Barcelona they understood. They got the message instantly and very graphically and understood what we were talking about. They deserve full marks for the way in which they've been able to embrace that.

It's a 60,000 seater to begin with, with the option to expand in the future. What needs to happen for that expansion to take place?

We're putting in the planning application for 60,000 because we already have an existing planning consent in Stanley Park for a 60,000 seater stadium. Clearly this is a radically different design so it does require a fresh application. We're trying to expedite the process by putting in an initial application for 60,000 which means we don't need to do too much additional work on transportation and environmental impact.

We're using the existing planning consent to a degree but our aspiration is very clear and that

is on the day we open we want to have a greater capacity than that. What we need to do is get started on site as soon as is practical. We're very much in the hands of the planners but once we get on site and the construction process starts then we'll look at putting a second planning application in so that over time we can address other concerns in a rather more measured way. The hope is by the time we open we'll have a greater capacity.

Are you hopeful it'll be 2010 when the new stadium opens?

Absolutely, that's very important. It sounds a long time away but it isn't with a project of this size. Obviously it's slipped a year from the original aspiration but I'm sure everybody will agree that the delay will be well worthwhile for the end product. We're very much hoping to hit 2010.

We've heard the word 'regeneration' many times over recent years – has that remained a key driver behind this new project?

Yes, very much so. As I've said, the design recognises the part the stadium plays in terms of the setting of the park. It's very clever the way that it now sits within and shows respect to the park. It's much closer to the existing stadium site

LIVERPOOL FOOTBALL CLUB   SOUTH WEST VIEW

LIVERPOOL FOOTBALL CLUB

and is aligned with it, so when the next stage of the redevelopment of Anfield Plaza takes place it'll be nicely integrated. It's our investment, which is £300 million plus, which we hope will be the catalyst for the community and the city in regenerating north Liverpool, which of course is long overdue.

How big a role will the stadium play within the community?

We've always been committed to the community partnership centre – the replacement for Vernon Sangster. That is absolutely in the plans and very much in our thoughts. That commitment is very clear. It's a spectacular stadium and it's certainly going to be a key factor in the regeneration of north Liverpool and it's something we hope the community will appreciate.

You've been involved in this project and the developing changes to it from day one – how happy are you with where we are now?

I'm really excited. It is fantastic and I just can't wait for it to be open.

With new players having arrived this summer and new stadium plans revealed today – this is a good time to be a Liverpool fan isn't it?

It's really exciting on and off the pitch. It's about having a world class club in every respect. We want to be world class on the pitch and hopefully we're progressing in that direction and there's no doubt that with a stadium like this that we'll be truly world class off it as well.

New Stadium

VIEW TO KOP

Rafa Benitez

The plans for the new stadium are absolutely fantastic. The design is really good, really pretty and really nice. For me the pitch is always what's most important and I'm sure that will be okay too. The facilities the new stadium will provide are going to ensure that the future of this club is a great one and this is what our fans deserve. It looks very different to other stadiums I have seen. There are a lot of windows and it really is ground-breaking in terms of stadium design. I'm sure it will be considered as one of the best in Europe. Unfortunately, I cannot play anymore so I won't be able to experience playing a match there but it would be fantastic for me to still be manager when we move and win lots of silverware there.

Steven Gerrard

To be honest I knew it was going to be great but after spending five minutes looking at the plans I was just completely blown away by it. It's amazing and the best thing about it, I think, is that it's so different to any other. We will have our own identity stamped all over this stadium and that's how it should be. We are Liverpool Football Club, we expect the best and this will be the best. I've played in some special stadiums but this is something special and it's so important that we are not seen to be copying another club. The fact that a massive Kop stand will be incorporated into the new stadium is great. As a supporter myself, I know what to look for in a stadium and I'm sure all our fans are going to love it. We all know the level of noise 40,000 Liverpudlians can make at Anfield so I can't even begin to describe what 60,000 plus can do inside the new stadium. It's going to be unbelievable and I can't wait to lead the team out there. The prospect of this was one of the major factors in me signing a long-term deal with the club and I just hope I'm still around when the day comes for us to play our first game in it.

Jamie Carragher

Everyone is excited by the new plans. They are spectacular. We've got a great stadium at the minute in Anfield, but the designers have come up with something completely unique and we thank them for that. I've never seen a football ground like it and that's what makes it so special. There are a lot of great stadiums across Europe but too many of them look the same nowadays. A club of our stature, tradition and history deserve something more than a general bowl-shape design so it's great for the designers to have come up with this. The fans will love it, especially when they see the plans for the new 18,000 seater Kop. That's going to be some stand. It's going to be modern and very hi-tech but it's good to see that tradition hasn't been overlooked. It'll have the feel of an old ground, with the four distinctive stands, but it'll be very much a new stadium. It provides me with the perfect motivation to remain at the top of my game because I want to still be in the team when we eventually move there.

Xabi Alonso

The plans are very impressive. I think it's important that the new stadium will be unique and have its own character, just like Anfield does at the moment, and from looking at the designs it certainly looks this way. It's not a traditional bowl-shape stadium and that is good. To keep four separate stands gives it an identity of its own and I think this is what catches the eye. Liverpool is famous for the atmosphere generated by its fans and from looking at the pictures I'm sure the new stadium will be just as atmospheric, if not more so. Anfield is really special, we all know that, but the new stadium will be a great one and I'm looking forward to playing there. It's going to compare very favourably with the best stadiums in the world. It looks different and special.

Steven Gerrard

Interview

Steven Gerrard believes the time has come for Liverpool to end their agonising wait for Premier League glory.

Not since 1990 has the league title come to Anfield and as a boyhood Kopite himself, the skipper is feeling the pain as much as anyone.

"Winning the league this season has got to be a priority for me, the manager, the players and the new people in charge," he said.

"It's been a long time since this club won the league and we have to improve in the Premier League and give it a better go.

"Since the takeover happened you can feel the optimism, you can feel the fans' excitement and the players and staff are no different - we are all looking to the future with great optimism.

"This team will be strengthened and then it's down to the players to perform and earn the right to be title contenders. The fans have been hugely supportive but now it's time for us to deliver."

Gerrard is satisfied with the progress being made at the club over recent seasons, with two Champions League finals in three years clearly demonstrating the quality already at Anfield.

But he now wants to see Liverpool's tremendous form in Europe transferred to the weekly demands of English football's top flight.

"We're a very good side in Europe," he said. "In one off games or over two legs we can beat any team out there and we have proved that on a number of occasions. We are a very, very dangerous team to play against but we know where we need to improve.

"What we achieved last season in the Champions League was fantastic, even though it was heartbreaking to lose the final in Athens. The boys were down at the end of the night and that's only to be expected, but I am confident this team will reach another European final. There's not a doubt in my mind about that because the way we play is suited to that type of football. What we have to do now is repeat it in the Premier League and that's the big challenge which lies ahead."

And Gerrard believes manager Rafael Benitez's decision to remain at Anfield can only help the Reds achieve their long term goals.

"He's one of the best in the business so of course it's great news that he's said he wants to stay with us," he said. "Rafa lives and breathes football and we know we are lucky to have him at our club.

"He's said he's staying, a lot of the boys have signed longer contracts and the boss has strengthened the squad over the summer so I believe we are in good shape to move forward at the pace we all want to.

"As a Liverpool captain and as a fan I am absolutely desperate to win the Premier League. Like a lot of the lads here, it's the one trophy I haven't won in my career and I dream of the moment when I can lift it above my head.

"I've had the pleasure of lifting the Champions League trophy and that was the best moment of my footballing life, but if we win the league then it will equal that achievement.

"I know how much the fans want it because I feel the same myself. It's what drives us all on. We want to be successful and we want to win a lot of trophies. We've done it in the Cups over a number of years and now the aim is the title.

"It won't be easy because there are a number of top quality sides also sharing the same dreams, but the important thing for us this year is to be competitive because it's a long time since we actually put together a genuine bid for the league."

Road to Athens

Liverpool 2-1 Maccabi Haifa
Third qualifying round, first leg

Our European journey began with a tie billed by many of the players as the toughest qualifier Liverpool had ever faced – and that's how it turned out. Anfield was stunned by a first-half opener from Gustavo Boccoli, and it needed a couple of debutants to turn things around. Craig Bellamy levelled things following a weak parry from Nir Davidovitch before Mark Gonzalez hit a sensational 88th minute winner.

Maccabi Haifa 1-1 Liverpool
Third qualifying round, second leg

Security concerns meant the Reds were spared a daunting trip to Israel, though a trek to Kiev was hardly something for the Liverpool squad to look forward to. Things were made a little more comfortable when Peter Crouch nodded home a Jermaine Pennant cross to put the game just about beyond doubt. There were a few hearts in mouths when Roberto Colautti snatched one back nine minutes later, though it was the Merseysiders who progressed to the lucrative group stages.

Bordeaux 0-1 Liverpool
Group phase one

Peter Crouch headed the club to its 150th win in Europe as the Reds maintained their unbeaten start to the competition. The England striker had already narrowly missed two glorious chances but made no mistake from Craig Bellamy's right-sided corner on 58 minutes.

Liverpool 3-0 Bordeaux
Group phase one

Liverpool wrapped up their place in the last 16 with two games to spare thanks to a brace from Luis Garcia and skipper Steven Gerrard's first strike of the season. The visitors' miserable night was compounded when midfielder Fernando Menegazzo saw red for a second-half head butt on John Arne Riise.

Liverpool 2-0 PSV
Group phase one

Rafa Benitez fielded a full-strength side in a bid to secure top spot in Group C, and though his objective was achieved, it came at a price Peter Crouch and Steven Gerrard claimed the goals which ensured – in theory at least – an easier second round draw, but the evening was marred by injuries to Xabi Alonso, Mark Gonzalez and Jermaine Pennant.

PSV 0-0 Liverpool
Group phase one

Liverpool opened their Group C account with a useful point against the Dutch champions. The visitors were unlucky not to fly home with more, with Dirk Kuyt and Stevie G both striking the woodwork in the second half.

Liverpool 3-2 Galatasaray
Group phase one

Europe's comeback kings nearly got a taste of their own medicine after taking a 3-0 lead through Luis Garcia and Peter Crouch. But just when it seemed like game-over, Anfield was rocked by a pair of quick-fire headers from substitute Umit Karan. Fortunately, Rafa's normally watertight defence regained its composure to see out a victory which left the 2005 champions top of Group C.

Galatasaray 3-2 Liverpool
Group phase one

In 2005 three goals in six minutes and an impressive comeback assured the Ataturk Stadium's place in Liverpool's European Cup folklore. On this second visit to the stadium the Anfield diehards wouldn't have enjoyed seeing Jerzy Dudek concede three on Turkish soil once more, albeit in a glorified friendly, though a brace from Robbie Fowler would at least have brought a smile to their faces.

Road to Athens

Barcelona 1-2 Liverpool
Second round, first leg

So much for an easier second round draw! The Gods conspired to hand Liverpool the toughest possible second round tie – reigning champions and everybody's favourites to once again lift the trophy in Athens, Barcelona. It looked like Barca could run away with it early on, Deco's opener helping to inspire the kind of fluid football for which the Spanish giants have become famed. The gods then contrived to make heroes out of John Arne Riise and Craig Bellamy, the players at the centre of the pre-match controversy, and it was Liverpool who'd head into the second leg as favourites to make the quarter-finals.

Liverpool 0-1 Barcelona
Second round, second leg

A late goal from Eidur Gudjohnsen may have given Barcelona a win on the night, but Rafa's reputation for masterminding faultless European performances remained very much intact. Ronaldinho, Eto'o and Messi barely had a sniff thanks to the colossal Jamie Carragher and his brigade. A special night could have been even more memorable had the crossbar not come to Victor Valdes' rescue to deny both John Arne Riise and Momo Sissoko in the first half.

PSV 0-3 Liverpool
Quarter-final, first leg

Liverpool may have been handed, on paper at least, the easiest quarter-final draw, but football's not played on paper. The Dutch champions had already disposed of Arsenal, and Rafa Benitez attempted to extinguish any complacency by reminding his players that it was PSV coach Ronald Koeman – then manager of Benfica - who shattered their Champions League dreams just 12 months previous. The trick seemed to work. Goals from Steven Gerrard, John Arne Riise and Peter Crouch all but secured our place in the semi-finals with 90 minutes to spare.

Liverpool 1-0 PSV
Quarter-final, second leg

With a titanic semi-final tie against Chelsea just about secure, Rafa took the opportunity to rest big-guns Steven Gerrard and Jamie Carragher. Another Englishman, Peter Crouch, bagged the only goal of the game.

Chelsea 1-0 Liverpool
Semi-final, first leg

Cheered on by their flag-waving hoards, Jose Mourinho's men made it advantage Chelsea going into the second leg at Anfield. Joe Cole opened the scoring from close range after a marauding run from the impressive Didier Drogba.

Liverpool 1-0 Chelsea (4-1 on pens)
Semi-final, second leg

In 2005 Anfield played host to what is widely regarded as one of it's greatest European night when the champions of England were sent packing in front of an atmosphere the like of which had not been witnessed before. The repeat couldn't match that, could it? Well yes, it could

actually. Daniel Agger's first-half strike from a gorgeously-worked free-kick helped tee up a dramatic period of extra-time in which Dirk Kuyt looked to have sealed it for the Reds – only for his strike to be wrongly ruled out for offside. What came next (Rafa's crossed legs, the boos which accompanied Frank Lampard's long walk to the Anfield Road end and Pepe's penalty heroics) will live long in the memory of every Liverpool fan in every corner of the globe.

AC Milan 2-1 Liverpool
Final

Liverpool's European dreams were shattered inside Athens' Olympic Stadium as Filippo Inzaghi's double helped Milan exact revenge for their Istanbul misery two years earlier. A deflected free kick on the stroke of half time and then a clever finish from Kaka's pass put the Rossoneri on their way to victory, although Dirk Kuyt did revive hopes of an Istanbul-style comeback with a close range header two minutes from time. In the end it was too little too late for Rafa's Reds, as our hopes of claiming a sixth European Cup were extinguished in ancient Greece.

Pepe Reina
Interview

Pepe Reina has admitted the prospect of playing for Liverpool in their brand new stadium helped convince him to pledge his future to the Reds.

The Spanish goalkeeper penned a new five year deal in the summer of 2007 which will keep him at Anfield until at least 2012, and with the new ground set to open two years earlier it means Reina should have plenty of opportunities to play his football in the club's new home.

"It did go through my mind when I was talking about a new contract," he said. "In an ideal world we'd stay at Anfield because it offers so much as a stadium, but we all know that for a number of reasons we have to move.

"The chance to play for Liverpool in their new stadium is something we can all look forward to and I am sure it will be a spectacular place when it's finished."

There were other reasons, of course, why Reina decided to prolong his stay on Merseyside – not least his belief that the Reds are perfectly poised to make a genuine challenge at the top of the Premier League table over the coming years.

"I spoke with Rafa and his thoughts for the future really excited me," he said. "He has ambitions for the team which I want to be part of and I'm sure the other players feel the same. The idea now for all of us is to keep winning matches and to challenge for titles. That's what we'll be looking for.

"Our fans deserve the league title and that's what we'll be looking for. Seventeen years without winning it is far too long for this club and that's why our biggest target this year has to be the Premier League.

"I am very happy with this contract. It was always my wish to sign a new deal because this is a good club which is looking forward to a very ambitious and attractive project.

"The details of the contract were very straightforward. Rick Parry and the American owners made everything easy and in the end it was a good solution for the club and a good solution for me."

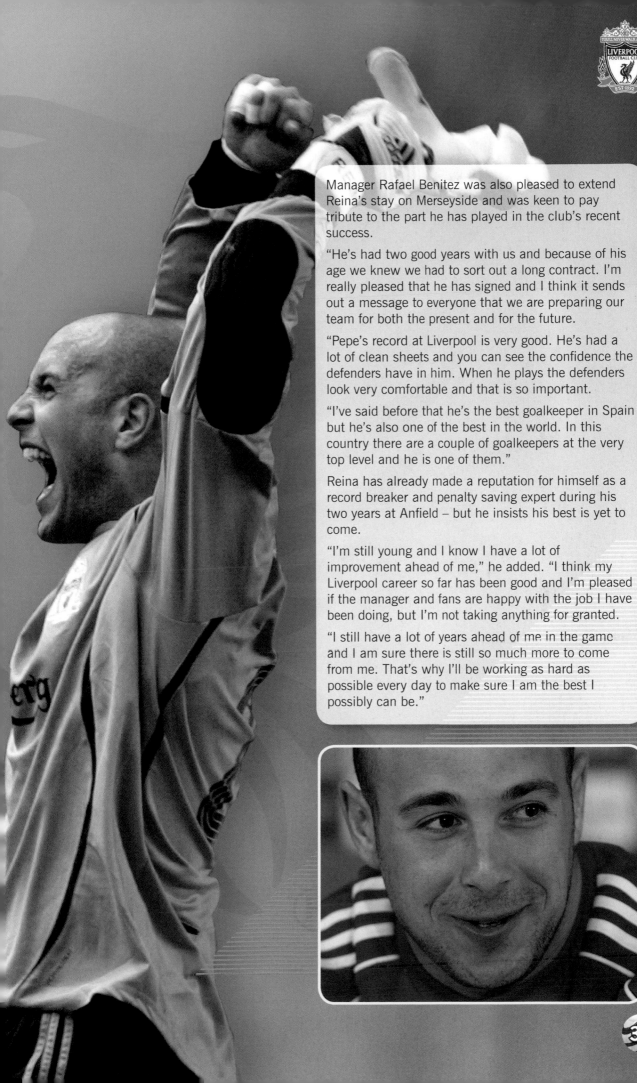

Manager Rafael Benitez was also pleased to extend Reina's stay on Merseyside and was keen to pay tribute to the part he has played in the club's recent success.

"He's had two good years with us and because of his age we knew we had to sort out a long contract. I'm really pleased that he has signed and I think it sends out a message to everyone that we are preparing our team for both the present and for the future.

"Pepe's record at Liverpool is very good. He's had a lot of clean sheets and you can see the confidence the defenders have in him. When he plays the defenders look very comfortable and that is so important.

"I've said before that he's the best goalkeeper in Spain but he's also one of the best in the world. In this country there are a couple of goalkeepers at the very top level and he is one of them."

Reina has already made a reputation for himself as a record breaker and penalty saving expert during his two years at Anfield – but he insists his best is yet to come.

"I'm still young and I know I have a lot of improvement ahead of me," he added. "I think my Liverpool career so far has been good and I'm pleased if the manager and fans are happy with the job I have been doing, but I'm not taking anything for granted.

"I still have a lot of years ahead of me in the game and I am sure there is still so much more to come from me. That's why I'll be working as hard as possible every day to make sure I am the best I possibly can be."

Club Quiz 2008

01 In which country was Javier Mascherano born?

02 From which club did Liverpool sign Dirk Kuyt?

03 Who scored Liverpool's winning penalty in the 2006 Champions League semi-final second leg penalty shoot out victory over Chelsea?

04 Daniele Padelli left the Reds at the end of the 2006-07 season to return to which club?

05 Who scored Liverpool's final goal of the 2006-07 league campaign?

06 Youngster Nabil El Zhar has represented which country at under-20 level?

07 Who is Liverpool's reserve team manager?

08 How many penalties did Pepe Reina save in the shoot-out success over Chelsea in the Champions League semi-final?

09 Who was the only team to beat us in the league at Anfield last season?

10 Who scored a hat-trick in the excellent Premiership victory over Arsenal?

11 — Who wears squad number 25 at Anfield?

☐☐☐☐ ☐☐☐☐☐

12 — From which club did Liverpool sign John Arne Riise?

☐☐☐☐☐☐

13 — Which country does Steve Finnan represent?

☐☐☐☐☐☐☐☐☐ ☐☐ ☐☐☐☐☐☐☐

Daniel Agger's first goal for Liverpool came against which side?

14 — ☐☐☐☐ ☐☐☐

Which club did Rafael Benitez manage before coming to Liverpool?

15 — ☐☐☐☐☐☐☐☐☐

Emiliano Insua made his first team debut against which side?

16 — ☐☐☐☐☐☐☐☐☐☐☐

Who scored our winning goal in the Nou Camp against Barcelona last season?

17 — ☐☐☐☐ ☐☐☐☐ ☐☐☐☐

Who netted two goals for Milan against Liverpool in the Champions League final?

18 — ☐☐☐☐☐☐☐ ☐☐☐☐☐☐☐

Against which side did we win our first away game during the 2006-07 season?

19 — ☐☐☐☐☐

20 — Sami Hyypia plays for which international side?

☐☐☐☐☐☐☐

Xabi Alonso

Interview

Xabi Alonso had one overriding reason why he wanted to resist interest from other European clubs to remain a Liverpool player - his desire to be involved in Rafael Benitez's 'exciting project'.

The Spanish midfielder thrilled his army of supporters when deciding to commit his future to the club last summer, especially as speculation in the newspapers was beginning to suggest his time on Merseyside might be drawing to a close.

But Alonso insists he always intended to pen a new deal and now can't wait for the good times to keep arriving at Anfield.

"I knew there was interest from other clubs but it was always my idea to stay here," said Alonso.

"I have been here for three seasons now and have such special feelings for the club and the supporters. I understand what Liverpool FC means to so many people. It is such a special club and I just didn't want to leave.

"We agreed that the talks would take place after the Champions League final and, to be honest, in the end it was a simple decision for me because I could see right away that the attitude of the club towards me was spot on.

"I greatly appreciate all the hard work that Rick Parry put in on the contract and the faith that Rafa Benitez has shown in me. We all wanted to reach an agreement and we're all happy with the outcome.

"I want to be part of what lies ahead because I know it is going to be exciting. I've signed for another five years and there's no reason why we can't be successful.

"It's also good news to see that other players have signed new contracts. Stevie, Carra and Pepe are all big players for us and it's great they have all shown their commitment. I'm sure the manager will be bringing in new players as well and that the new owners will be making a big effort to improve the squad."

Alonso admits Liverpool under achieved to a certain extent last season but he's confident the same mistakes won't be made this time around.

"We know where we went wrong last season and where we need to improve," he added. "We made such a poor start to the campaign and at this level you can't afford to do that if you have any hopes of being successful.

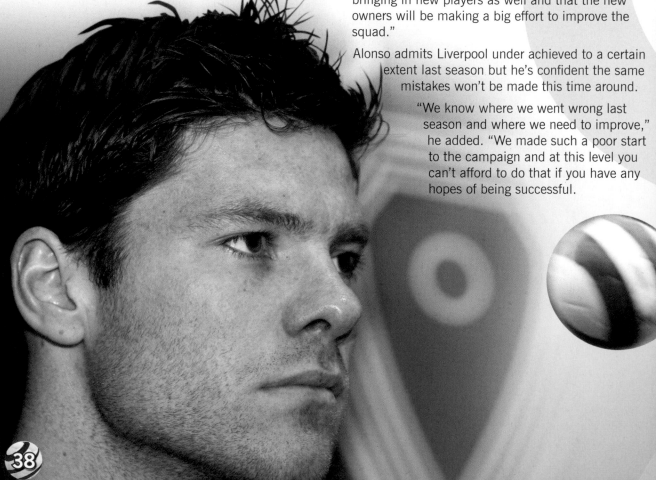

"We lost points where we shouldn't have lost them and we know how important it's going to be to make sure we're much better in those games this season.

"I'm not saying we're going to win this or we're going to win that, but I do know we can compete with anybody on our day and we all share the same goals and ambitions. We want to win trophies and we want to be successful. That's why we play the games and that's why the fans come to watch us. It's up to us to deliver. We know we're good enough."

And Alonso is confident he will have a big part to play in the club's future, despite the manager's increased options in the centre of the field.

"It's great to have competition and I am ready to fight for my place," he said. "The more top quality players we have then the better the level of the team will be. I'm confident I can play a lot of minutes on the pitch and keep the confidence of the manager."

Trivia Corner
Did you know...

Appearances

Most first team appearances	Ian Callaghan (857)
Most League appearances	Ian Callaghan (640)
Most FA Cup appearances	Ian Callaghan (79)
Most League Cup appearances	Ian Rush (78)
Most European appearances	Jamie Carragher (91)

Youngest/Oldest/Longest

Oldest player	Ted Doig, 41 yrs & 165 days v Newcastle United (A), 11 April 1908
Youngest player	Max Thompson, 17 yrs & 129 days v Tottenham Hotspur (a) 8 May 1974
Most seasons as an ever-present	Phil Neal (9)
Most consecutive appearances	Phil Neal (417) 23 October 1976 to 24 September 1983
Longest serving player	Elisha Scott – 21 yrs & 52 days: 1913 to 1934
Oldest debutant	Ted Doig, 37 yrs & 307 days v Burton U (H) 1 September 1904

Goals

Most first team goals	Ian Rush (346)
Most League goals	Roger Hunt (245)
Most FA Cup goals	Ian Rush (39)
Most League Cup goals	Ian Rush (48)
Most European goals	Michael Owen (22)
Highest scoring substitute	David Fairclough (18)
Most hat-tricks	Gordon Hodgson (17)
Most hat-tricks in a season	Roger Hunt (5 in 1961-62)
Most penalties scored	Jan Molby (42)
Most games without scoring	Ephraim Longworth (371)
Youngest goalscorer	Michael Owen, 17 yrs & 144 days v Wimbledon (a) 6 May 1997
Oldest goalscorer	Billy Liddell, 38 yrs & 55 days V Stoke City (h) 5 March 1960

Internationals

Most capped player	Ian Rush (67) with Wales
Most international goals	Ian Rush (26)

Honours

Most medals	Phil Neal (20)

Matches

Record victory	11-0 v Strømsgodset
Record defeat	1-9 v Birmingham City

Jamie Carragher
Interview

Jamie Carragher signed a new contract committing himself to Liverpool until 2011 and immediately declared: " We have to win the league."

Carragher is delighted with the success the Reds have enjoyed on the European stage over recent seasons, but he realises the size of the challenge which lies ahead if Liverpool are to regain their place at the top of English football.

And he believes it's this season which will help shape the club's future success in the Premier League as Rafael Benitez's new look squad looks to challenge Chelsea and Manchester United at the top of the table.

"It's a very similar situation to 2002," explained Carragher. "Gerard Houllier had done really well for three years and that was the summer everyone was looking for us to push on, but unfortunately it didn't work out.

"When a manager first comes to a club, no-one can expect to win the title straight away but by the second or third year you hope to have built the foundations of a team that can challenge. I think we had that then and we've got that now, and this is where we'll be looking to do more.

"Rafa has done brilliantly well since he came here but it's fair to say everyone will be looking for us to close that gap at the top now. That last step is always the hardest. If we don't improve from this point we'll just go sideways rather than upwards and that's not going to be good enough if we're going to challenge Manchester United and Chelsea.

"It's harder than I can ever remember as a player or supporter to win the league. Chelsea and United have raised the level, and the top four managers are probably the best four managers in the world.

"The club couldn't have done much more over the last few years because we've done everything apart from win the league. I'm desperate to do that over the course of this contract and I know everyone else here feels the same."

Carragher had no hesitation when a new contract was put before him after the Champions League final and he's thrilled with the prospect of playing the whole of his footballing career with one club.

"I've always said I wanted to stay here for the rest of my career," he said. "Hopefully I've got one more [contract] left in me that will take me until the end of my career. I have signed for four years and hopefully I can still be a regular in the team.

"My other aim is to still be in the team by the time we get to the new stadium. I think it's going to be brilliant for everyone - the players, the club and the supporters. I want to be a regular for Liverpool by the time we get to a new stadium.

"We're definitely moving in the right direction as a club. We've been in two European Cup finals in three years. I think we have put the club right back up there in European terms. You can't expect to win the European Cup every year but you've got to be there or thereabouts every year and that is starting to happen.

"We are getting to semi-finals and finals and we are knocking on the door every year. That's what Liverpool is all about. That's what it's been about in the past and I think over the last two or three years, we have got Liverpool back up there. We have also won the Super Cup twice and the UEFA Cup in 2001 so it has been a great few years for Liverpool in Europe. We would love to go close to that again but, as I say, each year you want to be knocking on the door which is what we've done."

Players on –
Champions League Final

Jamie Carragher:

"We are devastated but hopefully the defeat will make us stronger and we will be back next season.

"While it's hard to take losing a final, at the same time we've got to hold our hands up and give great credit to AC Milan who are a great side.

"We enjoyed the celebrations of winning it two years ago so we have a lot of respect for Milan and we will move on from this.

"Their first goal was a bit fortuitous and I should have cleared the ball better than what I did and it then put Xabi Alonso under pressure to clear the ball. At this level the smallest detail counts.

"I didn't think there was much in the game and we had a good chance with Stevie but unfortunately we couldn't score.

"I didn't think Milan had a lot of chances and I thought we played very well in the second half but no-one will remember that and it's Milan's night.

"I thought we handled Kaka as well as any team has done in this tournament and Mascherano put in a few great challenges on him. He set up their second goal but he is always going to cause any team problems because he is the best player in the world.

"Our fans were probably the man of the match again and full credit to them. We are just devastated we couldn't bring the cup back for them."

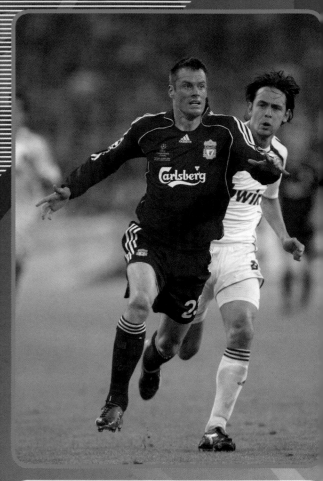

Jermaine Pennant:

"We had some chances in the first half, myself included, and if we had taken them it would have been a different game," said Pennant.

"Stevie G had a good chance in the second half but it wasn't to be for us. I feel we can take a lot of heart from our performance and we didn't have much luck on the night.

"You have to say the manner of which they scored the first goal was a killer blow to us because it was a cruel deflection and Pepe went the other way.

"We kept plugging away and got a late goal that gave us a little bit of hope but then they just got everyone back and shut up shop.

"Getting to two Champions League finals in three seasons is a good achievement and shows how good a team we are, but next season we want to do better in the league and get closer to challenging Manchester United and Chelsea for the title."

Xabi Alonso:

"The difference between the two teams on the night was their goal at the end of the first half which was a lucky goal for them," commented Alonso.

"It was tough to take conceding a goal like that because we had played well in the first half. We had some good chances but couldn't score and they had most of the luck on the night.

"We scored a goal late in the game that gave us some hope but unfortunately it came too late to make a difference.

"It is not a nice feeling losing a final but back in 2005 we were celebrating after beating them. All we can do is say congratulations to them and now think about the future.

"Once again our supporters were fantastic. They are always behind us and that's what makes it the more disappointing that we couldn't bring the cup back for them.

"What we have to do now is challenge for the Premier League title. Always you can improve and we need to be more consistent in the league."

Steven Gerrard:

"You've got to take it on the chin, move on and try to pick yourself up but at the moment it's heartbreaking," he said.

"I thought we started well, we were in control just how we like to be but when you do that you've got to score. They got the first goal, with a bit of luck, but it was a big lift for them.

"We gave everything but it wasn't to be tonight and certainly this feels the complete opposite to what it was like after Istanbul."

Dirk Kuyt
Interview

Dutch striker Dirk Kuyt is promising the best is still to come after an impressive first season in the Premier League.

The highly rated striker has already made a massive impression since arriving from Feyenoord in the summer of 2006 - but he isn't ready to rest on his laurels and has insisted Liverpool fans have yet to see him reach his top form.

"I believe in what I can offer to the side and I believe my best performances are still ahead of me," he said. "I'm a team player first and foremost and winning games is all that matters, but at the same time I want to make a contribution to the team and help us be successful.

"I've really enjoyed my career with Liverpool so far, firstly because this is such a special club to play for and also because English football is so exciting. I knew when I came here that it was going to be a great challenge and I'm enjoying every second of it.

"I got off to a good start and I think the fans enjoyed my performances, but the important thing now is to step up a level. Everyone at the club knows we need to improve if we want to challenge for or win the title, and for that to happen we need to increase our performance levels week after week."

Kuyt's performance levels have been much admired since his first display in a Liverpool shirt way back last August 2006 against West Ham United. His introduction as a second half substitute was followed by an all action display which immediately endeared him to the hearts of the Kopites.

But away from football Kuyt is also an inspiration for thousands of youngsters who don't enjoy anything like the same priviliges as the modern day footballer.

Eighteen months ago Kuyt set up the Dirk Kuyt Foundation, a charitable organisation which aims to improve the lives of some of the third world's poorest people in places like Nepal and Ghana, as well as in Holland's inner cities.

"It is good to try to help," he says. "Footballers are fortunate because we are paid good money for doing something that we enjoy. I just think that when it is possible I should try to give something back because I am aware that not everyone is as fortunate as I am.

"Whenever the collectors came to my door looking for donations for charity I always gave money but I just felt that I could do something more, that maybe a footballer could help something happen in one year that might otherwise have taken five.

"A photographer I know told me about the children in Nepal and I wanted to help them straight away. From that point we went on to set up the foundation and it is going well.

"Basically, we funded the building of a house for the children in Nepal to live in and I become the 'father' of the house and my wife Gertrude is the 'mother'.

"I have a contract with Adidas and whenever I do commercials with them I give the money to the foundation. I also have a Dirk Kuyt clothing line on the Internet where people can buy t-shirts, caps and socks and all the money from this is also given to the foundation.

"Education is very important. If I wasn't a good football player, I would have given everything to studying. I don't see what I'm doing as special. It is just about giving something back."

Songs From The

You'll Never Walk Alone

When you walk through a storm
Hold your head up high
And don't be afraid of the dark
At the end of the storm
Is a golden sky
And the sweet silver song of a lark

Walk on through the wind
Walk on through the rain
Tho' your dreams be tossed and blown
Walk on, walk on
With hope in your heart
And you'll never walk alone
You'll never walk alone

Fields of Anfield Road

Outside the Shankly Gates
I heard a Kopite calling
Shankly they have taken you away
But you left a great eleven
Before you went to heaven
Now it's glory round the Fields of Anfield Road.

All round the Fields of Anfield Road
Where once we watched the King Kenny play
(and he could play)
We had Heighway on the wing
We had dreams and songs to sing
Of the glory round the Fields of Anfield Road

Outside the Paisley Gates
I heard a Kopite calling
Paisley they have taken you away
You led the great 11
Back in Rome in 77
And the Redmen they are still playing the same way
All round the Fields of Anfield Road
Where once we watched the King Kenny play
(and he could play)
We had Heighway on the wing
We had dreams and songs to sing
Of the glory round the Fields of Anfield Road

A Liverbird upon my chest

Here's a song about a football team
The greatest team you've ever seen
A team that play total Football
They've won the league, Europe and all.

A Liverbird upon my chest
We are the men, of Shankly's best
A team that plays the Liverpool way
And wins the championship in May

With Kenny Dalglish on the ball
He was the greatest of them all
And Ian Rush, four goals or two
Left Evertonians feeling blue

A Liverbird upon my chest
We are the men, of Shankly's best
A team that plays the Liverpool way
And wins the championship in May

Now if you go down Goodison Way
Hard luck stories you hear each day
There's not a trophy to be seen
'Cos Liverpool have swept them clean

A Liverbird upon my chest
We are the men, of Shankly's best
A team that plays the Liverpool way
And wins the championship in May

Now on the glorious 10th of May
There's laughing reds on Wembley Way
We're full of smiles and joy and glee
It's Everton 1 and Liverpool 3

A Liverbird upon my chest
We are the men, of Shankly's best
A team that plays the Liverpool way
And wins the championship in May

Now on the 20th of May
We're laughing still on Wembley Way
Those Evertonians are feeling blue
It's Liverpool 3 and Everton 2

A Liverbird upon my chest
We are the men, of Shankly's best
A team that plays the Liverpool way
And wins the championship in May

And as we sang round Goodison Park
With crying blues all in a nark
They're probably crying still
at Liverpool 5 and Everton nil.

A Liverbird upon my chest
We are the men, of Shankly's best
A team that plays the Liverpool way
And wins the championship in May

We Remember them with pride
Those mighty reds of Shankly's side
And Kenny's boys of '88
There's never been a side so great

A Liverbird upon my chest
We are the men, of Shankly's best
A team that plays the Liverpool way
And wins the championship in May

Now back in 1965
When great Bill Shankly was alive
We're playing Leeds, the score's 1-1
When it fell to the head of Ian St John

A Liverbird upon my chest
We are the men, of Shankly's best
A team that plays the Liverpool way
And wins the championship in May

On April 15th '89
What should have been a joyous time
Ninety six Friends, we all shall miss
And all the Kopites want justice (JUSTICE)

Red and White Kop

On a Saturday afternoon
We support a team called Liverpool
And we sing until we drop
In a red and white Spion Kop
We all live in a red and white Kop
A red and white Kop
A red and white Kop
We all live in a red and white Kop
A red and white Kop
A red and white Kop
In a town where I was born
Lived a man who sailed the seas
And he told me of his pride
They were a famous football team
So we trailed to Anfield Road,
Singing songs of victory
And there we found the holy ground,
Of our hero Bill Shankly
We all live in red and white Kop...

Poor Scouser Tommy

Let me tell you the story of a poor boy
Who was sent far away from his home
To fight for his king and his country
And also the old folks back home

So they put him in a Highland division
Sent him off to a far foreign land
Where the flies swarm around in their thousands
And there's nothing to see but the sands

In a battle that started next morning
Under an Arabian sun
I remember that poor Scouser Tommy
Who was shot by an old Nazi gun

As he lay on the battle field dying dying dying
With the blood gushing out of his head (of his head)
As he lay on the battle field dying dying dying
These were the last words he said...

Oh... I am a Liverpudlian
I come from the Spion Kop
I like to sing, I like to shout
I go there quite a lot (every week)

We support the team that's dressed in Red
A team that we all know
A team that we call Liverpool
And to glory we will go

We've won the League, we've won the Cup
We've been to Europe too
We played the Toffees for a laugh
And we left them feeling blue - Five Nil!

One two
One two three
One two three four
Five nil!

Rush scored one
Rush scored two
Rush scored three
And Rush scored four!

Fernando Torres

Interview

Fernando Torres arrived at Anfield amid a blaze of publicity in July and immediately told the Liverpool fans: "I'll fulfil your dreams!"

The 23 year old broke off his love affair with home town club Atletico Madrid - for whom he had averaged more than a goal every three games - to join the Rafa-lution at Liverpool as the club's record signing.

He admits leaving Madrid was a difficult decision to make - but in the end the lure of Anfield was simply too irresistible.

"I know the expectations are extremely high and I know that people are really keen to see me score lots of goals," said Torres. "Well, I'm just as keen to fulfil all their hopes and desires.

"I don't see it as a problem settling into any style of play, I think I can adapt to any sort of circumstances.

"The main thing is I'm coming here very positive, wanting to settle in as quickly as possible and work very, very hard to make sure that all people's expectations are fulfilled.

"Liverpool as a club doesn't need to be sold to any player – any player in the world would be proud to come here as an individual.

"So the confidence that had been shown in me by the club and manager from the very first time I spoke to him, that was enough to open all the doors in terms of coming here.

"I don't think adapting to the style of play will be a problem. I've watched English football a lot in great detail and I'm aware that refs let a lot more go in this country and it's harder to get a free-kick here than in Spain.

"I've also spoken to other players who play here at the club currently so I'm well prepared and it doesn't hold any fears for me."

He added "It has been a difficult decision to leave my all-time club. But it would have been hard for me to reject Liverpool's offer. It is a big leap for me and I think it was the right thing for everyone. It's one of the best, if not the best, clubs in Europe.

"I was aware of offers from other clubs but as soon as I knew Liverpool were interested I said to Atletico: 'Look, please listen to this offer.'

"There were many clubs being bandied around. Offers go directly to Atletico, so I wouldn't necessarily know about them, but as soon as I heard about Liverpool I told them Anfield was the only place I was interested in.

"Why? Because I'm aware of the history and how special this club is. The tragedies that have happened have made the bond between the fans and the club so strong. Liverpool just ticks all the boxes for me.

"There's team spirit and a desire to win instilled by Rafa, and then there's my new teammates like Pepe and Xabi. They, as well as Luis, have always spoken very positively about life here in Liverpool.

"A club like Liverpool has the opportunity to sign almost anybody in the world of football so news of their interest fills you with a lot of surprise, and at the same time a lot of pride.

"This was just an outstanding opportunity to join one of the best clubs in Europe. It's a team with a winning mentality and a fantastic history.

"You don't get opportunities like this every day of your life and it was a train I couldn't let go by.

"I decided this was the moment and the confidence shown in me by the manager and the club was important. All those things were important in my decision."

Torres' affection for Liverpool became apparent towards the end of last season when his captain's armband at Madrid came loose to reveal the Reds' motto 'You'll Never Walk Alone' emblazoned on it.

"It came from my mates," he smiled. "We're all Liverpool fans and have been for some years, so a few years back now the lads all got a tattoo on their arms.

"Obviously as a footballer I couldn't really get the same thing done myself, so what they did was on my last birthday they gave me a birthday present of the armband with 'We'll never walk alone' written underneath."

Fernando Torres

Rafa on Torres

Rafael Benitez believes Fernando Torres has all the qualities to be an even bigger hero on Merseyside than he was in Madrid.

The Spanish striker broke the hearts of his adoring fans at Atletico Madrid when deciding to sign for Liverpool in the summer and Benitez is confident his new 23 year old signing will soon establish himself as a Premier League star.

"Torres was the captain at Madrid, he was the icon, he was the leader," said Benitez. "He can do similar things now we have brought him here.

"He will have a really good relationship with the supporters because he can play physically with passion.

"If you know the supporters of Atletico Madrid, they are really good and always behind the club.

"He was seven years playing at Atletico. Everybody was talking about him all the time after every game. He knows what pressure is because Atletico is a big club.

"But I'd like to think we can improve him a lot. It's clear he can improve. He has this potential and he wants to improve."

He added: "Last year Atletico weren't playing in the Champions League or in Europe but he was always there fighting.

"In the last two games of the season he had an ankle injury and he was limping but he still played because he wanted to put his team in the UEFA Cup.

"Sometimes players now will have an injury and say 'okay I cannot play' but he was talking with his doctor and fighting for his club.

"He knew we were really interested but he wanted to give 100% for his former club.

"When I talked to him, he talked about his determination to move here and learn things and also to fight for trophies. All these things for me are really important."

Steve Finnan

Interview

Steve Finnan is banking on Liverpool firing on all cylinders from the start of the new season as the Reds look to mount a genuine challenge to bring the championship back to Anfield.

The top prize in English football has been away from the trophy cabinet since 1990 and the Republic of Ireland defender is mindful of the need for a good start to help build momentum for this season's Premier League assault.

It took the Reds until December to win an away game last season and Finnan knows that sort of statistic can't be repeated if our title hopes are to remain alive in the second half of the campaign.

"We made mistakes last season and let too many silly points slip away and that can't happen again," he said.

"The aim every year is to win the league because that's what everyone at the club wants so much, but these days it's easier said than done and you certainly can't do it if you're throwing away games you should be winning.

"We know what the standards are at Liverpool and we know what the supporters want. Over recent years we've enjoyed the cup successes and obviously we're pleased with what we've achieved in Europe, but now is the time to have a real go at the title. We were never in contention after losing so many away games early on last season. After that we had too much to do and although we got ourselves together and performed better in the second half of the campaign, in the end the damage had already been done.

"It would be great for the club if we could be up among the top teams from the start this time around and not have to play catch up too much. The league table starts to tell a story around Christmas time and then you can see who is likely or not likely to be involved at the end. Our aim this year is to make sure we have a say in the Premier League race."

Despite admitting the club's focus this season lies firmly on a title challenge, Finnan isn't giving up on any hopes of more European success at Anfield.

"Obviously we've done well in the Champions League over the last few years and I think teams across Europe now know what we are capable of," he said.

"To win in Istanbul was brilliant but then of course to lose in Athens was disappointing for everybody. We've experienced the highs and the lows of Champions League finals now and there's no doubting which emotion we want to go through again.

"It's a tough competition to win and it's great credit to the manager for taking us so far twice in three seasons. The question now is can we go for both of the main competitions and I'm sure we can. The boss knows what he is doing and he will be trying his best to put together a squad which is good enough to challenge for every competition we enter this season.

"Last year was a bad one for us in terms of the domestic cups but in the end we reached the Champions League final so maybe it worked out for the best. We never want to lose games though, so the aim will always be to win all the competitions.

"The standard in this country and in European football is getting higher and higher every year because better players are coming in and clubs are getting more money to spend. Everyone is stepping up a level and we're no different.

"We're definitely good enough to achieve more success this year and end the season celebrating with a trophy or two."

Andriy Voronin
Interview

We first heard of your move to Liverpool at the start of this year – how good did it feel to arrive?

It felt very good, of course. I am pleased to be here finally. I am very excited to be at a new club, and especially one where all the players and staff are so friendly. I've noticed how the atmosphere here is really good. The club is helping me and my girlfriend find somewhere to live.

You've played in Germany since you were a teenager, why was now the right time to move to England?

After being in Germany for 12 years I felt it was time for a change, and then even more so when the offer came in from Liverpool. It's such a famous and big club – one of the most famous in the world. You can't resist an offer like that. The task in front of Liverpool at the start of every season is to win trophies and I want to be part of that. I want to help Liverpool achieve things.

How much do you know about the club and its history?

Some, but I don't know all of it yet. I'm learning all the time though and I will soon be up to speed.

You played at Anfield for Leverkusen back in 2005. What was your impression of the club back then?

I will never forget that night, even though my team didn't perform as well as we could. Even for an opposition player, the supporters and the atmosphere in that stadium were unforgettable, and definitely the thing I remember most from that match. The Liverpool fans are world famous, and though this was not the only reason I decided to join this club, it was certainly one of the main reasons. I can't wait to play at Anfield in a red shirt.

What has Rafa told you about your role here?

As a striker, of course the main task for me is to score goals. That is my role.

How confident are you about forcing your way into the first team and becoming a success in English football?

I am confident. If I wasn't confident, I would not have made the decision to come here. I feel I can adapt and be a success in the English game.

Rafa on Andriy Voronin:

I am sure Voronin will be a good player for us. He has spent a lot of time in the German league and I know he is keen to take up this new challenge and prove himself in England.

He is a forward who will give us another option. He has very good game intelligence, he moves intelligently between the lines and he has a lot of quality.

It's always important for a manager to have a number of options all over the field and Voronin can certainly bring us something different in attack.

Summer Signings
Ryan Babel & Yossi Benayoun

Yossi Benayoun

First of all Yossi, how excited are you to be here?

I'm very excited. It's a big move for me. It's been a dream since I was a little child to play for one of the biggest clubs in the world and so I'm very happy.

Was it a difficult decision to leave West Ham?

To tell you the truth it was very difficult because I had a very good relationship with the people there and they treated me very well. It was hard to leave but when I heard of Liverpool's interest I couldn't say no. I explained to West Ham that this was my dream and I'm very grateful to them for letting me go.

Was it the case that it was Liverpool who were after you and so you felt you had no option but to say yes?

Yes, absolutely. I told West Ham I would only leave them to sign for Liverpool. I had another three clubs after me but I wasn't interested. When Liverpool came in I had to go.

Did you follow Liverpool when you were growing up as a young boy in Israel?

Yes, of course, and I'm also aware that two other Israeli players have played for the club in Avi Cohen and Ronnie Rosenthal. Everyone knows Liverpool in Israel, it's a big club and it's a dream for me to be here.

But Liverpool broke your heart very recently in an FA Cup final......

Don't remind me, I've been trying to forget about it!! I remember Steven Gerrard scoring in the last minute to make it 3-3. It was a lovely day for West Ham and for Liverpool and I enjoyed it very much.

What are your targets and ambitions now that you are here?

The main thing for me is to work hard, to try to do my best and to prove that I deserve to be here. These are the only things I'm thinking about at the moment.

Are you ready for the competition for places in Rafa's side?

Of course. When I decided to come here I knew I would be arriving at a club with more players, better players and more competition for places. I'm ready for the challenge, I believe in myself and I will try to do everything to prove what I am capable of.

What has the boss told you about the role you'll have to play here?

All he's said so far is that I must work hard and that everything will work out for me. That's all I am concentrating on.

As a Premier League player over recent seasons you'll be aware of how Liverpool are progressing under Rafa Benitez – what do you make of the job he's doing here?

Everyone can see that he is doing a great job. To play two Champions League finals in three seasons is a great achievement and now with the new players he has brought in I am sure we will have a better chance of going closer to winning the league title. He's done a very good job so far and hopefully we will keep improving under him.

What have you made of the summer's other signings?

We have brought in a lot of great players. I played against Fernando Torres when I was in Spain and I know he is a great player and I've also been impressed with Ryan Babel when I've seen him on television. They are two big players who are joining a lot of other big players who were already in the squad and I think we'll have a great team this season.

Is it realistic for Liverpool to win the Premier League title this season?

It's understandable that the fans want it so much because Liverpool are a club who should be challenging for all the trophies every season. All I can say is that we'll do everything we can to try and win the league this season and I know the fans will be behind us all the way. This club has one of the best sets of supporters in the world so we'll do everything to make it happen for them.

Is Anfield a stadium you've enjoyed playing at in the past?

It's unbelievable, really. The atmosphere during the game is a dream and I can't wait for my first moment on the pitch.

Ryan Babel

Ryan Babel is confident he will be able to make a quick transition from Dutch football to the Premier League and be a major success in England.

The Holland under-21 star signed in at Anfield over the summer, ending Rafael Benitez's long pursuit of the winger which stretches back to his days as Valencia manager.

The Reds' boss is delighted to have now landed his man and Babel is looking forward to showing why Benitez has been such a great admirer of his ability for such a long time.

"My target for this season is mainly to keep learning, know about England, know about the Premier League and know about the game here," he said.

"The fact that other players came in at the same time will probably help me too. I know it's going to be difficult and it takes time for players to settle in, but I believe I have the quality to do that, pick things up quickly and show what I can do in England.

"I'm still only 20 years of age and hopefully can get better, and with the likes of Steven Gerrard and Fernando Torres here, it's impossible not to learn from such great players. That's one of the reasons I chose to come to Liverpool, many of the guys have a lot of experience and I want to pick up on that and improve my game.

"I am settling in well and the boys in the squad have helped me a lot, especially Dirk. I know him from the Dutch national team and that is going to be important for me."

Babel insists he had no thoughts of leaving Ajax when the Dutch season came to an end last year, but one phone call to inform him of Liverpool's interest immediately changed everything.

"I was on holiday in Aruba and to be honest the only thing I was thinking about was being ready for the new season with Ajax. Then I heard rumours that Liverpool were interested and as soon as that became official there was no doubt in my mind where I wanted to go.

"I know about the Premier League because I watched a lot of the games on television and I am well aware that I have joined one of the biggest clubs in Europe. The fact Liverpool have reached two of the last three Champions League finals tells you they are building something good here and I want to be a part of it."

His new boss is thrilled at the prospect of having him in his ranks and spoke in glowing terms about Babel's qualities on the day he was officially unveiled as a Liverpool player.

"Babel is a player with pace, quality, great potential for the future and great ability for the present. He's played with Ajax in Europe and for the national team and shown what a good player he is," said Benitez.

"He was one of the best players in the (under-21) European Championships in the summer, but we've been watching him for a very long time. We first saw him when he was 16 when I was still at Valencia. We remember a game he played against Barcelona when he broke into the Ajax side and we've followed him ever since. There were a lot of big clubs interested in him. He is a very good player now, and in the future he could be fantastic.

"It's too soon when people start trying to make comparisons between him and Thierry Henry. Henry is a fantastic, experienced player who has shown his quality for a long time, but Ryan has all the assets you need to be a top player.

"He'll probably play more as a winger but the fact that he can play in both positions means he's a very valuable asset to us. It's good because with a player like him we can always change our plan depending on how a game is going."

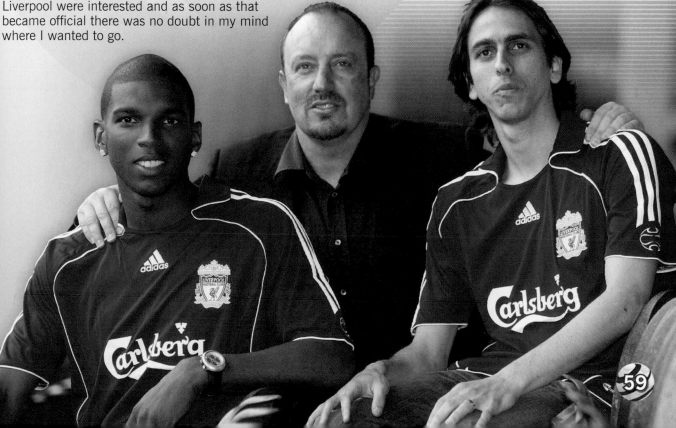

Quiz Answers

P36-37 Quiz Answers

1.	Argentina	8.	Two	15.	Valencia
2.	Feyenoord	9.	Manchester United	16.	Portsmouth
3.	Dirk Kuyt	10.	Peter Crouch	17.	John Arne Riise
4.	Sampdoria	11.	Pepe Reina	18.	Fillipo Inzaghi
5.	Harry Kewell	12.	Monaco	19.	Wigan
6.	Morocco	13.	Republic of Ireland	20.	Finland
7.	Gary Ablett	14.	West Ham		

P18 Word Search Answers

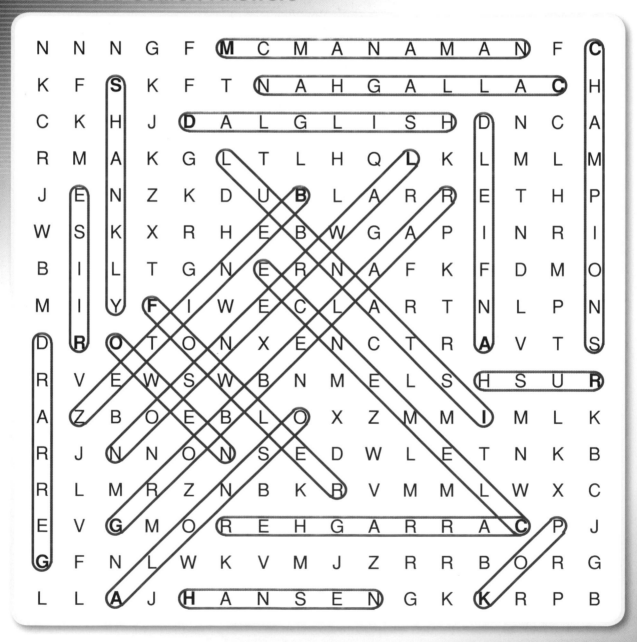

Spot The Ball

Was your skill and judgement good enough to find where the ball is? The answer is ball 'C'.